Table of Contents

Introduction

The different edge finishes and binding techniques taught in this book will widen your repertoire for finishing your quilts. To remove the fear factor, I suggest you make or purchase some prequilted fabric (to simulate a real quilt) and practice the different edge treatments on those samples. Write notes right on the samples for future reference. Practicing will allow you to relax and enjoy learning these new techniques, and you can refer back to the samples and notes anytime. All the stress is removed when you make *samples;* any mistakes you make are *learning experiences* and don't involve un-sewing, hair pulling, or tears!

Binding Secrets

The secret to binding a quilt and having the edge lie flat when finished is basting. Hand baste the edge of the quilt a scant ¼" (6mm) from the edge of the quilt before sewing on the binding. It can be basted with a walking foot and a long stitch on your machine, but I prefer hand basting. Basting the edge before binding prevents the layers from shifting. It also prevents the edge from rippling. It's preferable to hand baste the edge while the quilt is lying on a flat surface, such as a large table. You'll be able to see at a glance if the edge is lying flat.

Also, I never trim my quilt until *after* the binding is sewn on. If the edge doesn't appear to be straight, mark a straight line as a positioning guide for the binding or simply pull the binding straight as you are sewing it on. Once the binding is sewn on, go back and trim the backing and batting with scissors. Trim a couple of inches first, then check to see if you have allowed adequate batting and backing to "fill up" the binding. You easily can adjust the amount you trim off.

If you use cotton or wool batting (polyester batting can melt) steam press the edge of the quilt after the binding is finished. The edge will lie flat and straight.

Double Binding

Finished Width	Cut Size
¼" (6mm)	2¼" (5.5cm)
⅜" (1cm)	2½" (6.5cm)
½" (1.3cm)	3½" (9cm)
⅝" (1.5cm)	4¼" (11cm)
¾" (2cm)	4¾" (12cm)
1" (2.5cm)	6½" (16.5cm)

Note: A puffy or flannel quilt may need a wider binding.

Binding Choices

Double bias binding is generally recommended for use on bed quilts, as it wears better than either a single bias binding or a straight-of-grain binding.

If you are running short of binding fabric, or only binding a wall hanging, a single straight-of-grain binding is sufficient.

Single Binding

Cut the fabric strips 1¼" (3.2cm) wide for a single-fold bias or straight-of-grain binding. Sew a ¼" (6mm) seam for a ¼" (6mm) finished edge. If you'd like a wider single binding, take the finished width of the binding times 4 plus ¼" (6mm).

Double Binding

Cut the binding strips 2¼" (5.5cm) wide and sew a ¼" (6mm) seam for a finished double-fold bias or double-fold straight-of-grain ¼" (6mm) finished binding.

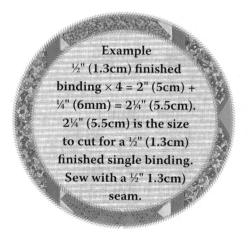

Example
½" (1.3cm) finished binding × 4 = 2" (5cm) + ¼" (6mm) = 2¼" (5.5cm). 2¼" (5.5cm) is the size to cut for a ½" (1.3cm) finished single binding. Sew with a ½" 1.3cm) seam.

TIP: Binding can be single- or double-fold, bias or straight-of-grain. It can match or contrast with the border. It can be narrow—¼" (6mm) finished, or wide, up to 1" or more. The choices are yours!

Cutting Bindings

Cutting Straight-of-Grain Bindings (Single- or Double-Fold)

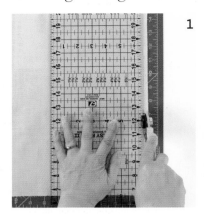

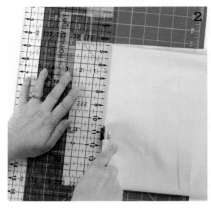

1 With the fabric folded, as it comes off the bolt, straighten the edge. Trim off selvages, as they may pucker in the quilt.

2 Cut strips the width needed for the binding. For the number of strips to cut, see formulas and table, page 5. Calculate the yardage for cutting binding.

TIP: It might be a wise idea to make the binding when the quilt top is completed, even before it's quilted. Sometimes there's a time lag (anything from a few days to a few years!) between finishing a quilt top and getting it quilted, and in the meantime the binding fabric could get lost or used in another project. Cut and prepare the binding when the quilt top is completed, then store them together, so when the quilting is finished you are ready to bind. The binding can be wrapped around a wide ruler or cardboard, then slipped off for flat storage.

Cutting Bias-Binding Strips (Single- or Double-Fold)

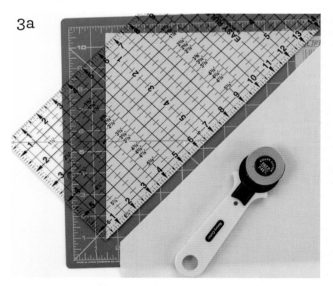

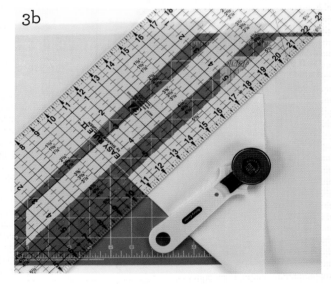

1 Trim both raw edges of the fabric piece. Trim off the selvages.

2 Open up the fabric so you are cutting only one layer. Cut off one corner at a 45° angle. (You have this marking on your ruler.) Align the 45° line with the short edge of your fabric and trim off one corner. (Discard the corner or save it for another project.)

3 Cut bias strips to the desired width. To facilitate cutting, fold over the 45° edge to shorten the cut.

Binding Formulas

To determine how much binding to make, add the measurement of the width of the quilt plus the length of the quilt and multiply by 2. Add 12" (30.5cm) extra for turning corners.

To determine how much binding to make for a scalloped or wavy edge, use the same procedure used for a quilt with straight edges; just allow one to two extra yards of binding. Or, to figure the measurement more accurately, "measure" with a length of string along the top and one side of the quilt, following the curves, then measure the string with a ruler and multiply by 2. Add 12" (30cm) for corners/ending.

To figure the amount of fabric for sraight-of-grain binding, divide the total length (see above) by 40" (101.5cm). Round up to the nearest whole number. This is the number of strips you need to cut. (Example: 252 ÷ 40 = 6.3 or 7.)

To figure yardage, multiply the number of strips by the binding width. Round up to the nearest ¼ yard (23cm) or ⅛ yard (11.4cm) (Example: 7 strips × 2½"(6.5cm) [binding width] = 17.5" (44.5cm) = ½ yard (46cm) or ⅝ yard (57.2cm).

To figure the amount of yardage needed for bias binding, see the Binding Table below.

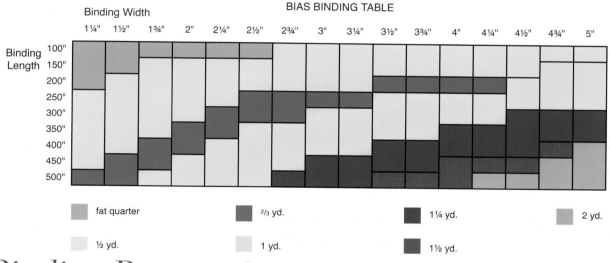

BIAS BINDING TABLE

Binding Width: 1¼" 1½" 1¾" 2" 2¼" 2½" 2¾" 3" 3¼" 3½" 3¾" 4" 4¼" 4½" 4¾" 5"

Binding Length: 100" 150" 200" 250" 300" 350" 400" 450" 500"

fat quarter   ⅔ yd.   1¼ yd.   2 yd.
½ yd.   1 yd.   1½ yd.

Binding Preparation

Joining square binding ends.

Joining angled binding ends.

Close-up of diagonal seam pressed open.

1 Whether single- or double-fold, bias or straight-of-grain, binding ends are joined with diagonal seams pressed open. This will reduce the "bump" in the binding when it is sewn to the quilt.

NOTE: When joining angled ends, offset the ends by ¼" (6mm). Sew from the V where the ends meet to the opposite V.

2 To make a double binding, either bias or straight-of-grain, fold the binding in half lengthwise with *wrong* sides together and press.

NOTE: Do not stretch the binding while ironing.

Sewing Bindings
Sewing a Single Straight-of-Grain Binding to a Straight Edge Quilt

Single straight-of-grain binding is sufficient for a small wall hanging or table runner. The small scale of the quilt does not call for a bulky binding, and the edge won't have heavy use, as in a bed quilt.

Single bias binding is a must when binding a scalloped, curved or shaped edge. Bias binding is necessary for curved edges, and single binding is a good choice for scalloped edges, as it eliminates some of the bulk in the *V* of the scallop. Yes, it will wear out more quickly than a double bias binding, but it will be much easier to sew on a scalloped edge.

To stitch a single or double straight-of-grain binding to a straight edge of a quilt, follow these steps:

1 Quilt as desired. Hand baste a scant ¼" (6mm) from the edge of the quilt to hold the layers together and keep them from shifting. See Binding Secrets page 3.

2 Match the raw edge of the binding to the raw edge of the quilt top. Start in the middle of one side, remembering to leave an 8" (20.5cm) tail. Stitch the binding with a ¼" (6mm) quilting foot, sewing a ¼" (6mm) seam (or wider if the strips are wider).

3 Miter the corners (see Mitered Corners page 7).

4 End the binding with a "Perfect Fit" binding technique (see page 8).

5 Trim the excess batting and backing.

6 On the top side of the quilt, press the binding away from the edge of the quilt to make the binding easier to fold.

7 Fold the binding under ¼" (6mm) and stitch down the binding by hand with single threads that match the binding. Stitch down with a blind hemstitch, making sure the stitches don't show on the front of the quilt.

TIPS: Use appliqué sharp needles for hand stitching the binding—they are thin needles designed for this type of stitching.

When stitching down the binding by hand, keep the body of the quilt away from you. Hold only the binding edge and you'll find it easier to stitch.

Use binding clips instead of pins to hold the binding edge down for sewing and you won't stick yourself!

Sewing a Double Straight-of-Grain Binding to a Straight Edge Quilt

Prepare the quilt edge by basting a scant ¼" (6mm) from the edge of the quilt. Prepare the double straight-of-grain binding by piecing together with diagonal seams pressed open, then pressing in half lengthwise with wrong sides together. (See Binding Preparation on page 5.)

A double straight-of-grain binding can be used for any straight quilt edge. A *bias* double binding is recommended for bed quilts because of its durability. To apply a double straight-of-grain binding, align the raw edges of the binding to the raw edge of the quilt. Start in the middle of one side and leave an 8" (20.5cm) tail. Stitch until you reach the corner; miter the corners. (See Mitered Corners on page 7.)

To end the binding, see "Perfect Fit" binding technique (page 8).

After the binding has been sewn on, trim off excess batting and backing and turn the binding to the wrong side. Stitch down by hand with thread that matches the binding. The binding should cover the line of stitching on the back side of the quilt. The hand stitches should not come through to the front of the quilt. See tips for stitching the binding down by hand (page 6).

Mitered Corners

1 To miter, stitch to within a seam's allowance from the corner (this could be ¼" (6mm) or wider, depending upon the width you have chosen) stop and backstitch.

2 Remove the quilt from under the presser foot and trim threads. Turn the quilt 90° to begin stitching the next edge of the quilt.

3 Fold the binding on the diagonal, pull it straight up, then fold back down, with the fold on the previous edge of the quilt.

4 This automatically builds in enough extra binding to turn the corner. When finished, you will have a nice mitered fold at the corner.

"Perfect Fit" Binding

To join the binding ends without a lump, and without being able to tell where you have started, follow these steps:

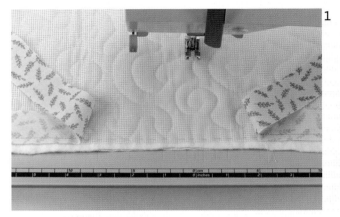

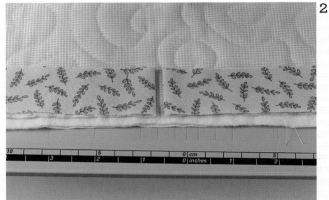

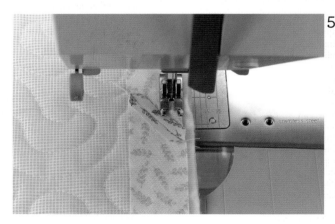

1 Start your binding in the middle of one side of the quilt. Leave an 8" (20.5cm) to 10" (25.5cm) space on the quilt between the beginning and end of the binding. Leave an 8" (20.5cm) tail at the beginning and end of the binding strip.

2 On a flat surface, have the binding ends meet in the center of the unstitched space, leaving a scant ¼" (6mm) space between them. Fold the ends under at that point.

3 Cut off one end at the fold. Then, using the end you have cut off (open it, if it is a double binding), use it to measure a *binding's width* from the fold. Cut off the second end at that point.

4 Join the ends at right angles with right sides together. Stitch a diagonal seam. Check to make sure the seam has been sewn properly, then trim to ¼" (6mm). Finger press and reposition the binding on the quilt.

5 Finish stitching the binding to the edge of the quilt.

Marking

Any curved or shaped quilt edge needs to be marked before binding. I recommend using a blue wash-out pen. (It allows you to change the markings.) Spritz with water, wait until it dries, and try again.

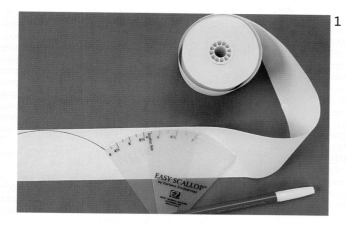

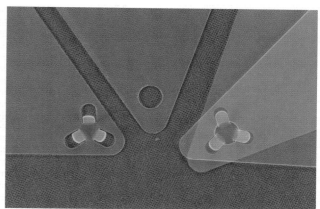

1 A way to preview a curved or shaped quilt edge is to cut a length of calculator tape the length of the side of your quilt. Mark the scallop, curved or shaped edge on the paper. Cut out and use as a template to mark your quilt edge.

2 You can mark a scalloped, curved or shaped edge with any lid, plate or bowl from your kitchen, or use a compass to achieve the right curve. A helpful adjustable tool designed specifically for marking scallops and curves is Easy Scallop.

3 The Easy Scallop must be assembled before first use. Bend the tabs at the bottom of one half of the tool up and insert through the hole on the matching piece. Flatten the tabs. Do the same for the remaining tool.

4 The Easy Scallop has a tab that locks it into place at a particular size. The tools are marked at ¼" (6mm) intervals and are easily adjustable from 4" (10cm) to 12" (30.5cm).

5 The scalloped, curved or shaped edge can be marked either before or after quilting. It can be a last-minute decision after the quilt has been quilted, or it can be marked before the quilting is done. Perhaps a quilting motif could be added into the curved edge shapes.

6 A scalloped border also can be made to fit the blocks in a quilt. Set the Easy Scallop (or mark intervals) the size of the finished block, centering the scallop over the block. The corner scallops will end up the width of the border and do not need to be the same size as the rest of the scallops.

Scalloped Edge With Rounded Corners

A scalloped edge is *not* difficult to mark. Follow this step-by-step procedure and you'll see just how easy it is.

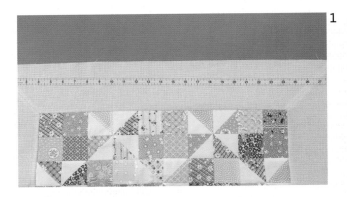

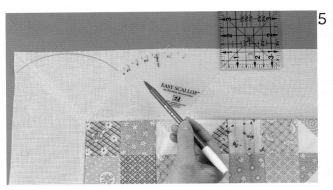

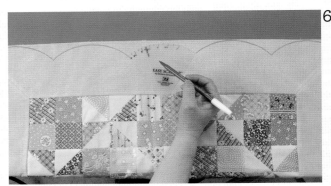

1 Measure the quilt border from edge to edge.

2 The next step is to choose the *number of scallops* you want to create. To do this, simply take your finger and "air draw" the scallops along that edge. How many scallops did you draw?

3 Take the length of the quilt edge and divide by the *number of scallops*. That will yield the *size* of the scallops.

4 Round the answer from step 3 to the nearest quarter inch (9¼" or 23.5cm). Set your Easy Scallop tool to that measurement. If not using Easy Scallop, move on to the next step.

EXAMPLE:
The quilt edge measures 54½" (1.4m).
I chose 6 scallops.
54½" (1.4m) divided by 6 = 9.0833.

5 Begin marking at the corner of the quilt. (You can mark right to the edge, as you will be sewing ¼" (6mm) below the marked line.) Mark the first scallop with Easy Scallop, making sure you have the same amount of indent at each end of the tool. If not using Easy Scallop, measure off increments of the size chosen in step 3, and mark the curve with a lid, plate or compass. (The trick is finding the right size.)

6 Mark scallops in the same manner from both corners toward the center, adjusting the middle scallop(s) as needed. The Easy Scallop tool is infinitely adjustable. If you find you have to adjust too much in the center, then go back and check your math—you probably didn't divide accurately. (Using the blue wash-out pen, spritz the line with cold water, wait until it dries, and try again.) Mark the *opposite* border in the same way.

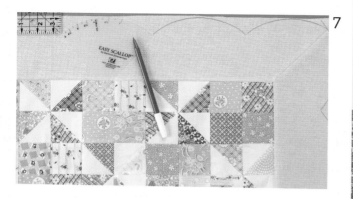

7

EXAMPLE:

The quilt measures 54½" (1.4m) x 76½" (2m). We've marked the 54½" (1.4m) top and bottom edge. To mark the side edges, I will choose 8 scallops (remember, I used 6 scallops at the top and bottom). 76½" (2m) divided by 8 = 9.5625. Set the Easy Scallop tool at 9½" (24cm) (or mark intervals at that size). Mark the remaining two sides of the quilt in the same manner as steps 5 and 6 on page 10. Notice you have automatically marked a rounded corner.

7 Usually a quilt is rectangular. If so, you need to refigure the size of the scallops for the remaining two borders. It makes sense that, since the two remaining borders are longer than the ones just marked, you will need one or more additional scallops along that edge. Follow steps 1 through 6 again. If the quilt is rectangular, the size of the scallop for the longer sides can be slightly different than the scallop size for the top and bottom of the quilt. As long as the scallop size stays within an inch (2.5cm) more or less of the first scallop size, it will look fine. The scallop sizes for the top and bottom of the quilt do *not* need to be the same as for the sides of the quilt, but they do need to be similar.

8 Do *not* cut on the marked line. This line is merely a *placement guide* for the binding. If you cut on the marked line, the quilt will have a bias edge, which would stretch, fray and distort. Leaving the extra fabric around the scallop ensures the edge is stable for sewing.

9 When the quilting is completed, baste on that marked line to prevent the layers from shifting when the binding is sewn on. You can hand baste or machine baste (use the longest stitch length) with a walking foot.

Binding a Scalloped Edge

The secret to binding a scalloped edge, without tears, is to use single bias binding cut 1¼" (3.2cm) wide. The binding needs to be bias to curve around the scallops, and the single binding is less bulky in the V's. A single binding is not as durable as a double binding, but consider this—the top layer of a double binding will wear out first and the binding will need to be replaced just as soon as a single binding.

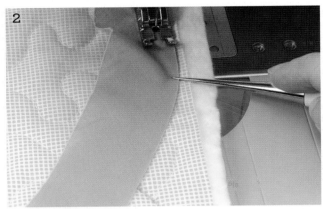

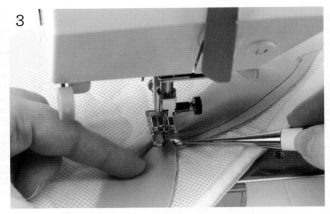

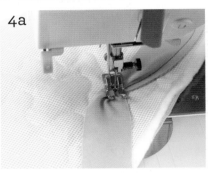

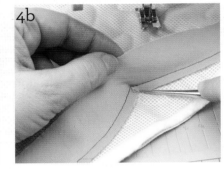

1 Baste by hand (or with a long stitch and walking foot on the machine) along the marked scalloped edge to keep the layers together.

2 Begin at the top of a scallop, leaving at least a 6" (15cm) to 8" (20.5cm) tail. Align the binding strip to the marked edge. Sew a ¼" (6mm) seam (use your ¼" [6mm] quilting foot for this task; you've basted, so no need for the walking foot). *Ease* the binding around the curves. Do not *pull*, as this will cause the scallops to cup.

3 Stitch to the bottom of the V, stop with the needle down, lift the pressure foot, and pivot the quilt and binding around the needle.

4 Push any pleats that form in front of the needle behind the needle with a stiletto or seam ripper. Making sure you don't stitch any pleats into the binding, lower the presser foot and stitch out of the V.

5 Continue around the quilt in this manner. Join the binding ends as shown on page 8.

6 Trim the backing and batting evenly, ¼" (6mm) from the stitching line. Do *not* clip the V, this will destabilize the scallops and make them floppy.

7 Pull the binding to the back side, tuck under ¼" (6mm) and stitch down by hand with matching thread. If you find that the scallop wants to "cup," you can steam the edges lightly to make them lie flat. (And, next time, you'll remember not to *pull* the binding around, but *ease* instead.) At the V, the fabric should just fold over upon itself to form a small pleat. This pleat will be more or less pronounced, depending upon the sharpness of the V. You can use a stiletto or the back of your needle to "help" in folding this pleat.

Scalloped Edge with "Ears"

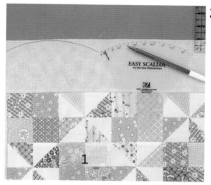

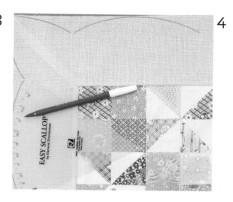

1 Measure the quilt edge. Choose the *number* of scallops. (See step 2 on Scalloped Edge With Rounded Corners page 10.) Divide the length by the number of scallops to determine the *size* of the scallops. (This is the same procedure you follow for the rounded corners on pages 10 and 11.)

2 Instead of starting with a full scallop at the corners, start with a *half* scallop at the corners. Make sure you have the same amount of indent at both ends of the scallop.

3 Mark from both corners toward the center as before. Adjust the center scallop(s) as needed. Mark opposite edges of the quilt the same way.

4 Repeat the same procedure for the remaining two sides, remembering to refigure and readjust the scallops if the length is different. (Refer to step 7 under Scalloped Edge With Rounded Corners on page 11.) Note that the "ears" will automatically happen at the corners.

5 When binding "ears," you will need to bind the corners of the quilt with a mitered corner. Refer to page 7 for detailed instructions for Mitered Corners.

Scalloped Edges with Square Corners

A third option for finishing the corners of a scalloped quilt is to leave them square. To do this, follow the directions for Scalloped Edges With Rounded Corners, pages 10 through 11, but only mark the *inside* of the scallop at the corners, leaving the corners square.

When binding, remember to miter the square corner.

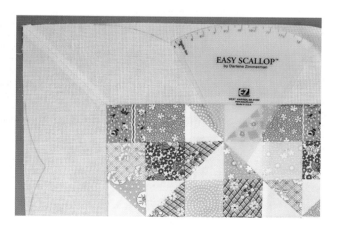

Notched Edge Finish

A scalloped edge adds a pretty touch to a quilt; often it gives a feminine look to the quilt. However, a notched edge can look masculine or have an Art Deco look.

A notched edge is simply a scallop with the top cut off, leaving just the *V* behind.

You can determine where you want the notches to be. They can be aligned with the blocks, or you can make notches the width of your borders and, possibly, in the center of each border as well.

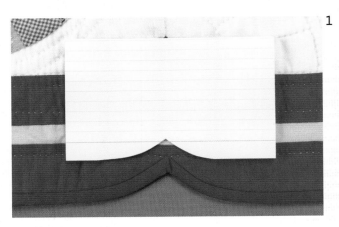

1 To mark the notches, make a template from a recipe card. Simply draw in a *V* shape, not more than a 90° *V* (as it would be too hard to bind) and about 1" (2.5cm) or less deep.

2 Bind with single bias binding, following the steps for binding a scalloped edge on page 12.

Free-Form Edges

For an art quilt, or a quilt with a contemporary look, you can design a wonderful free-form curvy border. Simply draw it freehand (remembering not to use more than a 90° angle in any *V*'s). Or you can use a tool called Flex Design Rule. It is a flexible ruler that you can bend (and it will stay) in any curvy shape, allowing you to design and mark a curvy border, and repeat it, if you choose to do so, on the remainder of the borders.

Bind a free-form border the same way you would bind any curved or scalloped border—with single bias binding.

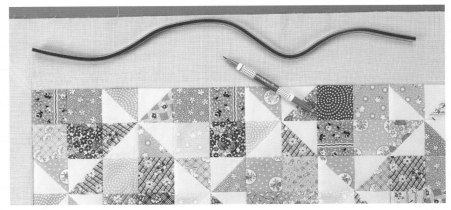

Curved Edge Finish—"The Wave"

A softly curved edge with rounded corners is perfect for a small quilt or baby quilt. It also will look quite lush and fancy on a bed quilt. Of all the curved edge finishes, you will find this one the easiest to bind, as there are no V's to pivot around.

To mark a curvy (wavy) edge you must choose an *uneven* number of scallops and use a rather *flat* curve.

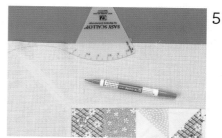

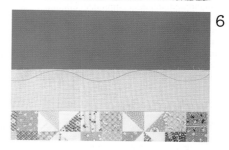

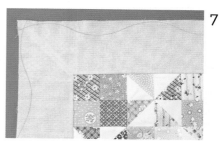

1 Measure the quilt from edge to edge.

2 Decide on the number of scallops (curves). Count both the inner and outer curves and remember to choose an *uneven* number.

3 Divide the length of the quilt by the number of scallops (curves). Round to the nearest ¼" (6mm). Set the Easy Scallop tool to that measurement (or, if not using the tool, move on to the next step).

4 Begin marking a full scallop at the edge of the quilt, keeping the same amount of indent on both sides of the tool.

5 Reverse the tool and mark an upside down curve. Check to make sure the indent is the same.

6 Repeat steps 4 and 5 at the opposite corner, working toward the center. Adjust the middle scallop (curve) as needed. Mark the opposite side the same way.

7 Measure, divide the length by the number of scallops (an *uneven* number) and mark the remaining two sides. You will have a softly rounded corner automatically marked.

8 Baste by hand (or by using the walking foot on the machine) along the marked line.

9 Bind with single bias binding cut 1¼"(3.2cm). *Ease* the binding around the inside and outside curves. Refer to Binding a Scalloped Edge on page 12.

Prairie Points

Prairie points must be added to the quilt *before* quilting. Prairie points are a surprisingly easy edge finish, but the proper sequence must be followed or you will have a big problem when you get to the last step.

Preparing the Prairie Points

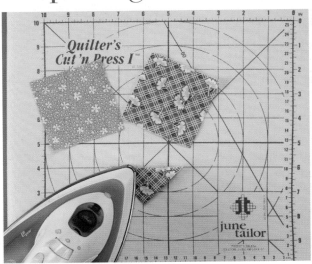

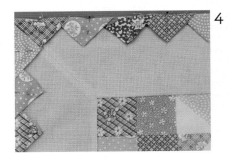

1 Cut squares from a variety of prints or the color of your choice. The square can be any size, generally from 2" (5cm) to 5" (12.5cm). Experiment with different size squares to find a size you like.

2 Fold a square once on the diagonal. Press. Fold again on the diagonal. Press. Repeat with each of the squares.

3 Tuck the folded end of one prairie point inside another, with at least ¼" (6mm) overlap at the base. (It can be more than ¼" [6mm].) Baste together with

a scant ¼" (6mm) seam (by machine, use the longest stitch) a continuous border of prairie points the length of your quilt edge. (At this point the quilt should *not* be quilted.) The prairie points should come exactly to the corners of the quilt top.

4 Sew the prairie points to the quilt top. Use a ¼" (6mm) seam, a regular stitch length and prairie points that just touch at the corners. At this point, the prairie points are all facing in toward the center of the quilt.

5 Layer, baste and quilt, staying about 1" (2.5cm) from the edge of the quilt. (Don't stitch over the prairie points.)

6 Lay the quilt on a flat surface and trim the backing and batting even with the raw edge of the quilt top (or, if you prefer more turn-under, cut ¼" [6mm] longer).

7 Trim the batting only, about ¼" (6mm) shorter than the quilt top.

8 Turn the prairie points to the outside of the quilt. The batting should tuck under the seam on the back side.

9 Turn the backing fabric under approximately ¼" (6mm), so that it covers the line of stitching. Trim excess bulk at the corners. Stitch down by hand with matching thread.

10 Finish any quilting along the prairie point edge if needed.

TIP: To make the prairie points fit the quilt edge exactly, remove a few basting stitches, adjust the prairie points closer or further apart, then re-baste. Do this as needed in several places.

Formula for Making a Continuous Prairie Point Edging

With this method, it is very important that the prairie point strip is exactly the length of your quilt top. It is *not* adjustable, as in the individual prairie point method. The prairie points made with this method are permanently connected. To ensure your prairie points fit your quilt, determine the length and the width of the strip and cut accordingly. The formula is as follows:

1 Measure the length of the quilt top; this is the **length** you will need to cut your strip. (You may need to piece the strip to get the proper length.)

2 Find a number between two and five that will divide evenly (or as close as you can get it) into the **length** of your strip.

3 Take that number × 2 to equal the **width** of the strip.

4 Measure, mark, cut and fold as directed on page 18, and finish according to the directions for a prairie point edge.

Continuous Prairie Points

This may be a method you never use, but make yourself a sample—you will impress your quilting friends.

When making prairie points all the same color or alternating two colors, you can use the following method to make them from a strip of fabric.

1 To make a *sample*, cut an 8" × 21" (20.5cm × 53.5cm) strip of fabric. Mark a line exactly down the center of the 21" (53.5cm) length of fabric strip.

2 On one half side of the strip mark off 4" (10cm) intervals.

3 On the other half of the strip, measure 2" (5cm) in and mark off in 4" (10cm) intervals.

4 Cut off and discard the 2" × 4" (5cm × 10cm) piece on each side. Cut up to the center on the remainder of the marked lines.

5 Fold the squares on the diagonal, first to the left, then to the right. Press.

6 Repeat for each of the squares, then tuck one inside the other, making a continuous line of prairie points. Baste a scant ¼" (6mm) along the base of the prairie points.

You can achieve another look with the prairie points by *not* tucking them at all. In that case, alternate prairie points will either be in front of or behind the others.

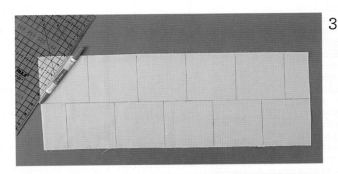

3

4

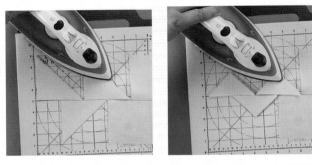

5

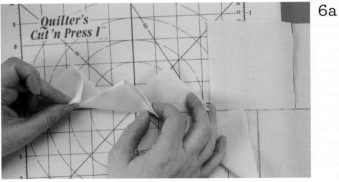

6a

6b

Knife-Edge Finish

The best option for a quilt with an irregular edge is a knife-edge finish. It is not hard to do, and it's an effective way to finish an irregular edge and keep it intact.

To make a knife-edge finish on *any* irregular edge, follow these steps:

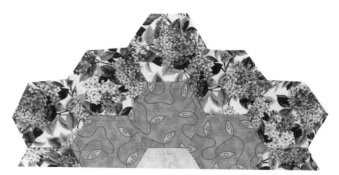

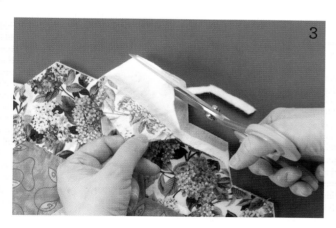

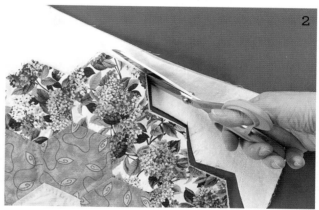

1 Leave the irregular edge until last. Layer, baste and quilt as desired, leaving the last row of hexagons around the edge unquilted.

2 Lay the quilt on a flat surface and trim the batting and backing even with the edge of the quilt top.

3 Trim the batting ¼" (6mm) *less* than the quilt top.

4 Fold the backing and quilt top edges in ¼" (6mm). The folded edges should just meet. Whipstitch the edges by hand with matching thread.

5 Finish any quilting along the edge.

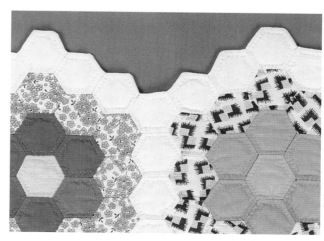

Ice Cream Cone Border

Ice cream cone borders are a unique edge finish found on 1930s-era quilts, most frequently seen on Dresden Plate quilts. Usually an ice cream cone border has a print alternated with a white or background upside down "cone."

The ice cream cones can be any length or width on the border of a quilt, and the angle can change. However, to make the border lie flat and straight (not curved) the ice cream cone and background cone pieces need to have the same angle. The angle can be whatever you choose. They can differ in width, but the angles of the two different cone pieces must be the same. You can use an acrylic tool to help you cut a 60° angle (or a different angle) for both pieces, or you can use the templates supplied on page 21.

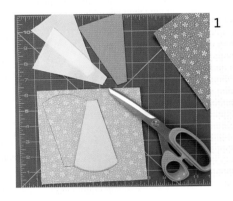

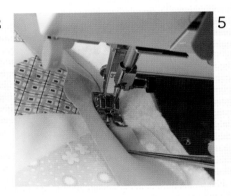

1 Ice cream cones can have flat or rounded edges, with the rounded edges being the most popular. Cut a print ice cream cone with the round template, and use background fabric with the flat top template.

2 Sew together with wide edges opposite one another.

3 There is no easy way to work out the mathematics of the ice cream cone border. You simply have to sew as many ice cream cones as needed for the border length. It is somewhat adjustable by taking in or letting out a few seams

across the border. Note that the corners do not make a right angle, but four cones together will fill out a corner.

4 Another way to adjust the ice cream cone border to fit your quilt is to add a wider inside border—either from the background color or a contrasting color. Cut the inside border a bit wider than needed, so you can trim evenly to make the quilt fit the border.

5 Once the border has been sewn to all sides of the quilt, you can layer, baste and quilt as desired. The gentle curve of the print ice cream cones forms a shallow scallop border. Hand baste a scant ¼" (6mm) along the outside edge to stabilize the bias edge and to keep the layers from shifting. Bind using a single bias binding. See page 12 for detailed instructions for binding a scalloped edge, and pages 4 and 5 for cutting and preparing a single bias binding.

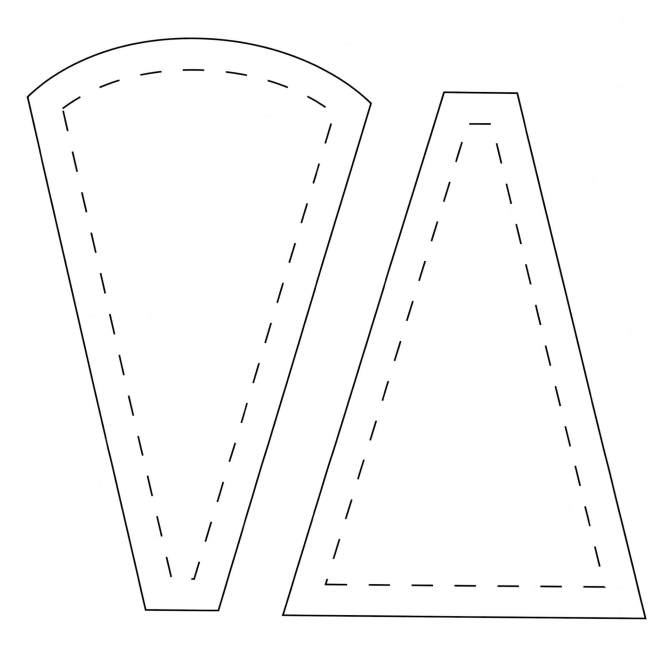

ICE CREAM CONE BORDER TEMPLATES

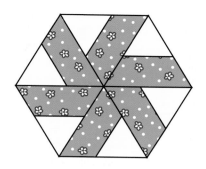

One simple shape is used in the construction of this quilt—a 60° triangle. You'll find it surprisingly easy to piece since there are no set-in seams. The extra triangles you cut from the strip sets can be used to make another quilt of any size.

Fabric Requirements

Vintage white: 2⅔ yards (2.4m)

Variety of prints: 15 fat quarters

Green (Aloe) solid: 1½ yards (1.4m)

Backing: 3 yards (2.8m)

Batting: Twin size

Cutting Directions

From	Cut	Yield
Vintage white	45—2" × 42" (5cm × 106.5cm) strips	90—2" × 21" (5cm × 53.5cm) strips for strip sets
From each print	6—2" × 21" (5cm × 53.5cm) strips	Strip sets
Green solid	10—3½" × 42" (9cm × 106.5cm) strips	116—3½" (9cm)—60° triangles*
	3—2" × 42" (5cm × 106.5cm) strips	Top and bottom borders
	7—1¼" × 42" (3.2cm × 106.5cm) strips	Binding

TIP

Finger press the strips before ironing. Keep the strip set straight, not curved.

Hollyhock Garden

Hollyhock Garden; 48½" × 56½" (123cm × 143.5m); 6" (15cm) blocks

Assembling the Blocks (Make 60)

Step 1: Sew the white and print 2" × 21" (5cm × 53.5cm) strips together to make 90 strip sets. Press toward the print strips.

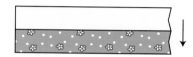

Step 2: Using the Equilateral 60° Triangle or template on page 26, cut A-triangles and B-triangles. Cut twenty-four A-triangles from each print. (Six A-triangles are needed for each flower.)

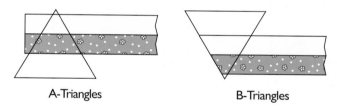

A-Triangles   B-Triangles

Step 3: Sew together three matching A-triangles, and press exactly as shown. No need to trim off the extended points (dog-ears). Instead, use the extended points to align the next unit. Make a second unit exactly the same and press.

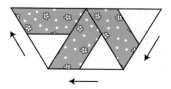

Step 4: Sew the two identical halves together to make a flower, matching up the extended points and the centers. Twist the center seam to open it, and press half the seam one direction, half the other (page 25). In the same manner, make a total of 60 flowers, one more than needed.

Assembling the Quilt

Step 1: Matching extended points, sew the green triangles to the upper left and bottom right corners, turning the hexagon flower units into diamonds. Sew only *one* triangle to the last ten flower units.

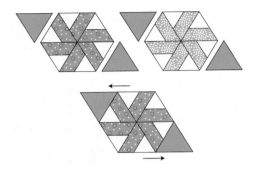

Step 2: Sew the flowers together in rows, pinning and matching the center horizontal seam. Twist the seam in the center to open so the seams go in opposite directions . Sew five rows with seven flowers, using the flower units with only one green triangle at each end as shown.

Step 3: Sew four rows with six flowers, adding an extra green triangle at each end as shown.

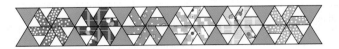

Step 4: Sew the rows together, pinning and matching at each seam intersection. Alternate the rows of seven with the rows of six. Press the seams all one direction.

Borders

Step 1: From the 2" × 42" (5cm × 106.5cm) green solid strips, piece border strips longer than necessary for the top and bottom of the quilt. Sew to the quilt, pressing toward the border. Trim off the border ends at the same angle as the flower blocks.

Finishing the Quilt

Step 1: Prepare the backing 3" (7.5cm) to 4" (10cm) larger than the quilt top. Trim the batting to approximately the same size as the backing.

Step 2: With the backing wrong side up, layer the batting, then the quilt top, right side up. Pin or thread baste the layers together.

Step 3: Quilt as desired. The quilt shown was machine stitched in the ditch between all the "petals" of the flowers. Each of the green triangles was hand stitched ¼" (6mm) from the seam. A small cable was quilted in the top and bottom borders.

Step 4: Before binding, hand baste a scant ¼" (6mm) from the edge of the quilt to hold the layers together and prevent shifting.

Binding

Step 1: Join the 1¼" (3.2cm) binding strips with diagonal seams pressed open.

Step 2: Sew the binding to the quilt with a ¼" (6mm) seam, matching the raw edge of the binding to the raw edge of the quilt top.

Step 3: At the inside corners, stitch to the bottom of the *V*'s, stop with the needle down, and pivot at the corner, pulling the quilt and the binding around the needle. Push the pleat that forms in front of the needle *behind* the needle. Lower the presser foot and stitch out of the corner, being careful not to stitch any pleats into the binding.

Step 4: At the outside corners, miter as usual.

Step 5: Join binding ends with the "Perfect Fit" binding technique.

Step 6: Trim excess batting and backing, turn the binding under ¼" (6mm), and stitch down by hand on the back side of the quilt with matching thread, covering the stitching line. At the V's, a little pleat should form on both the front and the back of the quilt.

Remember to sign and date!

Twisting the Seam

Try this trick whenever you have any type of four-patch unit. It will make the center seam intersection lie flatter.

Step 1: Before pressing the last seam on a four-patch, grasp the seam with both hands about an inch (2.5cm) 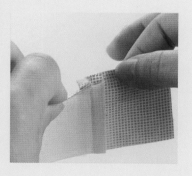 from the center seam. Twist in opposite directions, opening up a few threads in the seam.

Step 2: Press one seam in one direction, and the other seam in the opposite direction. In the center, 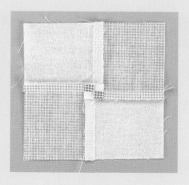 you will see a tiny four-patch appear, which lies very flat.

Hollyhock Garden
(Queen-Size)

Finished Size, 96" × 110" (244cm × 279cm), 8" (20.5cm) blocks. Set 12 × 13 for a total of 150 flower blocks.

Note: With the extra B triangles, you can make a second quilt. (You will need to purchase only another 4¼ yards [3.9m] of green.)

Fabric Requirements and Suggested Tools

Vintage White: 10½ yards (9.6m)

Variety of Prints: 50 fat quarters

   Green Solid: 4¼ yards (3.9m)

   Equilateral 60° Triangle (large template on page 26)

96" × 110" (244cm × 279cm) Cutting Directions

From the print fabrics, cut six 2½" (6.5cm) strips from each fat quarter for strip sets. You can cut three flowers (eighteen A-triangles) from each fat quarter or three A-triangles from each strip set.

From the white fabric, cut one hundred fifty 2½"× 42" (6.5cm × 106.5cm) strips to make three hundred 2½" × 21" (6.5cm × 53.5cm) strips.

From the green fabric for the triangles, cut twenty-five 4½" × 42" (11.5cm × 106.5cm) strips then cut into two hundred ninety-eight 4½" (11.5cm) triangles (see large template on next page or use the 4½" (11.5cm) size on the Equilateral 60° Triangle). For the borders, cut six 3½" × 42" strips (9cm × 106.5cm). For the binding, cut thirteen 1¼" × 42" (3.2cm × 106.5cm) strips.

Piece the strip sets and sew according to directions on page 23–24. Arrange in seven rows of twelve flowers and green triangles, alternated with six rows of eleven flowers.

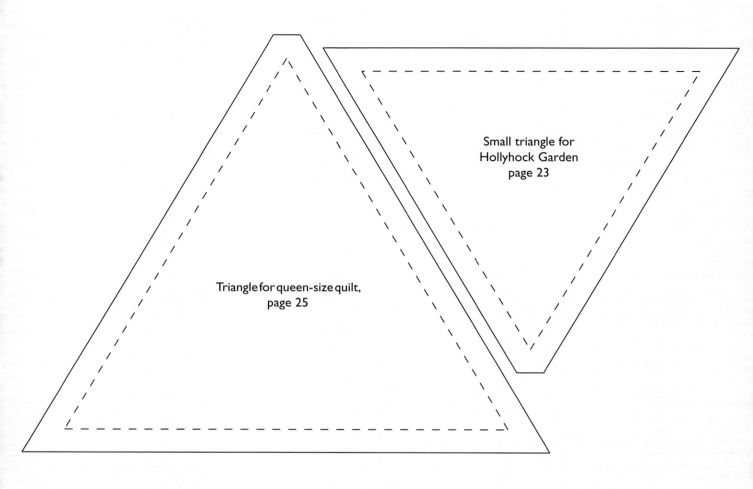

Small triangle for
Hollyhock Garden
page 23

Triangle for queen-size quilt,
page 25

Equilateral 60° Triangle

Step 1: Cut fabric strips according to the tool. For example, for a 3" (7.5cm) finished triangle, cut 3½" (9cm) strips. Position the triangle at the selvedge end of the strip with the chosen triangle height level with bottom of fabric strip. *The black tip of the triangle should be above the fabric strip.*

Step 2: Trim and discard the corner on the left side of the fabric strip. Cut along the right edge of the tool for the first triangle. Rotate the tool, align and cut again.

Step 3: Continue in the same manner to the end of the strip.

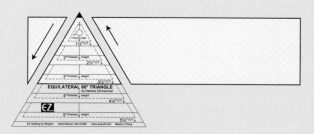

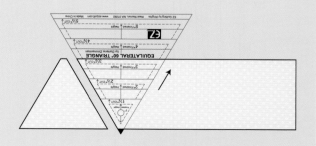

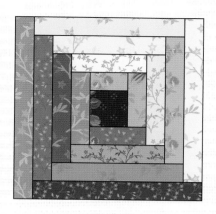

Fabric Requirements

Light prints: 16 fat quarters or scraps totaling at least 4 yards (3.7m)

Dark prints: 19 fat quarters or scraps totaling at least 5 yards (4.6m)

Block center: 1 fat quarter

Setting triangles and border: 4⅓ yards (4m)

Accent border and binding: 1⅜ yards (1.3m)

Batting: King size

Backing: 8¼ yards (7.5m)

Sweet Delights

Sweet Delights; 93" × 106" (236cm × 269cm); 10" (25.5cm) blocks

Flip-n-Set Tool

Step 1: With the tool open, find the *finished size* of the blocks to be set on point and cut strips to the width indicated on the tool.

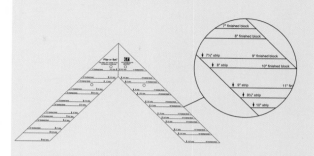

Step 2: Lay the tool on the *opened* strip with the point aligned at the top of the strip. Match the measurement line along the bottom of the strip. Cut on both outside edges of the tool for the first cut.

Note: The Flip-n-Set tool cuts generously sized triangles to allow for trimming.

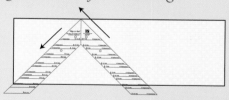

Step 3: Rotate the tool and align the point with the bottom of the strip and the edge of the tool with the edge of the fabric. Make the second cut.

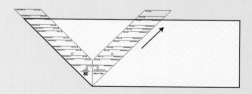

Step 4: Repeat, rotating the tool and cutting to the end of the strip.

Cutting Directions for Log Cabin Blocks

From	Cut	To Yield
Block center fabric	7—2½" × 21" (6.5cm × 53.5cm) strips	50—2½" × 2½" (6.5cm × 6.5cm) squares
Each dark fat quarter	8—1½" × 21" (3.8cm × 53.5cm) strips or total of 152—1½" × 21" (3.8cm × 53.5cm) strips	Cut 50 each— 1½" × 10½" (3.8cm × 26.5cm) 1½" × 9½" (3.8cm × 24cm) 1½" × 8½" (3.8cm × 21.5cm) 1½" × 7½" (3.8cm × 19cm) 1½" × 6½" (3.8cm × 16.5cm) 1½" × 5½" (3.8cm × 14cm) 1½" × 4½" (3.8cm × 11.5cm) 1½" × 3½" (3.8cm × 9cm) Cut largest sizes first.
Each light fat quarter	8—1½" × 21" (3.8cm × 53.5cm) strips or total of 128—1½" × 21" (3.8cm × 53.5cm) strips	Cut 50 each— 1½" × 9½" (3.8cm × 24cm) 1½" × 8½" (3.8cm × 21.5cm) 1½" × 7½" (3.8cm × 19cm) 1½" × 6½" (3.8cm × 16.5cm) 1½" × 5½" (3.8cm × 14cm) 1½" × 4½" (3.8cm × 11.5cm) 1½" × 3½" (3.8cm × 9cm) 1½" × 2½" (3.8cm × 6.5cm) Cut largest sizes first.

Log Cabin Block Assembly

Step 1: Starting with a block center and a light 1½" × 2½" (3.8cm × 6.5cm) rectangle, sew together and press toward the light rectangle.

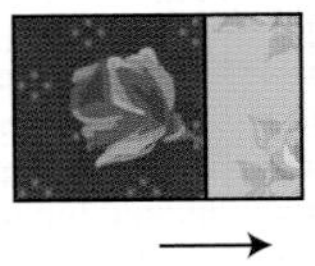

Step 2: Turn the block a quarter turn to the left (or counterclockwise) and sew a light 1½" × 3½" (3.8cm × 9cm) rectangle. Press toward the rectangle.

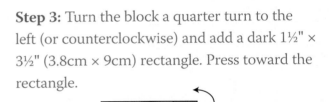

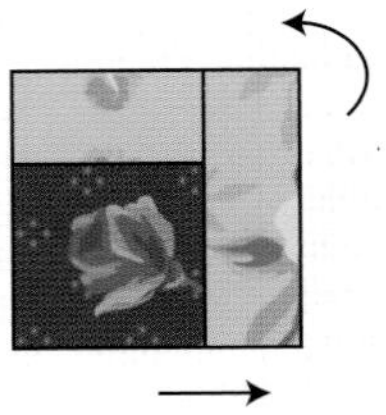

Step 3: Turn the block a quarter turn to the left (or counterclockwise) and add a dark 1½" × 3½" (3.8cm × 9cm) rectangle. Press toward the rectangle.

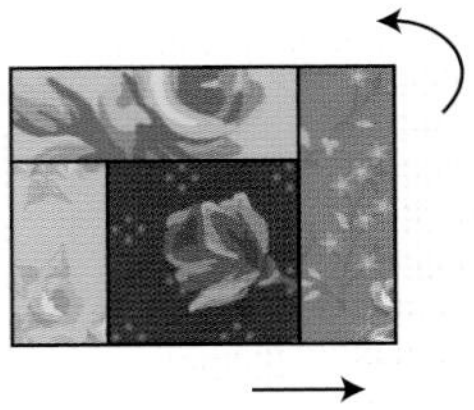

Step 4: Turn the block a quarter turn to the left (or counterclockwise) and add a dark 1½" × 4½" (3.8cm × 11.5cm) rectangle. Press toward the rectangle.

Step 5: Continue in this manner, turning counter clockwise and sewing two dark rectangles and two light rectangles to adjacent sides of the block, pressing after each addition. Make fifty blocks. At this point the blocks should measure 10½" × 10½" (26.5cm × 26.5cm).

Note: The rectangles have been cut the right length. If they don't fit properly, you will need to adjust your seam allowance to sew an accurate ¼" (6mm) seam.

Cutting the Setting Triangles

Step 1: From the setting triangles and border fabric, cut four 8" × 42" (20.5cm × 106.5cm) strips.* Open up the fabric strips and cut a total of sixteen setting triangles using Flip-n-Set tool.

Step 2: Cut one strip 9" (23cm) wide. From that strip cut two 9" (23cm) squares, cut once on the diagonal for corner triangles.

Step 3: Trim the remainder of the strip to 8" (20.5cm), and cut two more setting triangles with Flip-n-Set for a total of 18 setting triangles.

* If not using Flip-n-Set, cut five 15½" (39.5cm) squares. Cut each square twice on the diagonal for twenty setting triangles. You will only need eighteen setting triangles.

Assembling the Quilt

Step 1: Arrange the blocks in diagonal rows as shown. Use the setting triangles along the edges and the corner triangles at the corners.

Step 2: Sew the blocks together in diagonal rows, alternating the direction the seams are pressed in each row.

Step 3: Sew the rows together, matching and pinning seam intersections. Press all the row seams in one direction.

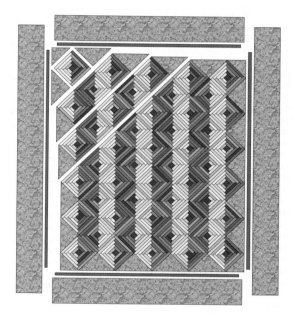

Sweet Delights **quilt assembly**

TIP: Setting triangles are cut slightly over size so you can straighten the edges of the quilt. To do this, lay a large square (or Flip-n-Set) over one corner. Mark a square corner with chalk or pencil. Repeat on each of the corners. Using a long ruler, connect the lines at the corners. Do not cut off the corners of the log cabin blocks! Trim the quilt to within ¼" (6mm) or more from the corners of the blocks. After you are satisfied the marks are as straight as can be, trim on the marked lines.

Borders

Step 1: From the accent border fabric, cut a total of nine 1½" × 42" (3.8cm × 106.5cm) strips. Join the strips with diagonal seams pressed open.

Step 2: Measure the quilt through the width. Cut two borders to this length and sew to the top and bottom of the quilt. Press the seams toward the borders. Repeat for the side borders.

Step 3: From the outer border and setting triangle fabric, cut four 10½"-wide (26.5cm) borders the length of the remaining fabric (or as wide as your fabric will allow).

Step 4: Measure the width of your quilt. Trim two borders to this measurement and sew to the top and bottom of your quilt. Press toward the borders just added. Repeat for the side borders.

Finishing the Quilt

Step 1: Cut the backing fabric into three equal lengths and sew together to make the backing. Trim the batting to the same size as the backing.

Step 2: Layer the backing wrong side up, the batting, and then the quilt top right side up. Baste.

Step 3: Quilt as desired. The quilt shown was machine quilted with feathers down the length of the quilt on the dark side of the blocks and in the ditch down the center on the light side of the blocks. Feathers were also quilted in the border.

Marking a Scalloped Border

Step 1: The top and bottom borders were marked using Easy Scallop set at a 10¼" (26cm) scallop. The sides were marked with a 10½" (26.5cm) scallop. The corners were rounded. Remember to mark from the corners to the center, adjusting the center one or two scallops as needed.

Step 2: Baste on the marked scallop line, but *do not* cut on that line. The basting will hold the layers together and prevent shifting while you sew the binding on.

Binding

Step 1: From the accent and binding fabric, trim off the selvages, then cut a 45° corner off the opened fabric. Set the corner aside for another project. Cut 1¼" (3.2cm) bias strips from the remainder of the fabric to total approximately 500" (12.7m). Join the bias binding strips with diagonal seams pressed open.

Step 2: Matching the binding edge to the marked line, sew a ¼" (6mm) seam allowance, stopping and pivoting at the V. (See page 12 for more instruction on binding a scalloped edge.)

Step 3: Following the instructions on pages 8, join the binding ends with the "Perfect Fit" technique.

Step 4: Trim excess batting and backing, turn to the back side and stitch down with matching thread. There is no need to clip in the V.

Sign and date!